DESERT

desert scorpion

NATIONAL GEOGRAPHIC NATURE LIBRARY

DESERT

NATIONAL GEOGRAPHIC NATURE LIBRARY

by Marfé Ferguson Delano

NATIONAL GEOGRAPHIC SOCIETY

Washington, D.C.

Sand dunes stretch to the horizon in Australia's Simpson Desert.

Table of Contents

Sonoran Desert

sand dunes

globemallow

caracal

lithop plants

the Gobi

Australian desert

gila monster

guanaco

Antarctica

WHAT IS A DESERT?

If you think a desert is nothing but dry, hot, sandy land, bare except for a camel or two, you are in for a surprise. Although deserts are definitely dry, they are not always hot and sandy, and most of them are far from empty. In fact, many of the world's deserts support an incredible variety of plants and animals, ranging from tiny insects to huge mammals—including camels, of course.

This book will take you to some of Earth's driest lands and introduce you to the plants and animals that call them home. Before we set off, fill your canteen, then start with these facts:

- A desert is a place that receives an average of FEWER THAN TEN INCHES OF RAIN (or snow) PER YEAR.

- Most deserts LOSE MORE MOISTURE through EVAPORATION than they get as rain.

- A typical desert has HOT TEMPERATURES at least part of the year.

- There are four basic kinds of deserts: SUBTROPICAL, COASTAL, RAIN SHADOW, and INTERIOR.

- Plants and animals that live in deserts have developed special features called ADAPTATIONS that help them survive.

fringe-toed lizard

land tortoise

6

sandgrouse

addax

caracal

fennec fox

scorpion

jerboa

7

Where in the World?

You can find the arid, or dry, lands called deserts in Africa, Asia, Australia, North America, and South America. All together, the deserts on these continents cover about one-fifth of Earth's land surface. The Arctic and Antarctic receive such low rainfall that they are sometimes called polar deserts. Because they remain cold year-round, however, these polar areas do not qualify as true deserts, which are hot at least part of the year.

pronghorn

saguaro cactus

Great Basin

Sonoran

Mojave

Chihuahuan

fennec fox

gila monster

rhea

Atacama

armadillo

Patagonian

Patagonian cactus

caracal

Bactrian camel

GLOBE-TROTTING
Deserts, indicated on this map in yellow, are not just scattered willy-nilly around the world. As you can see, most deserts lie in two globe-circling belts centered on imaginary lines called the Tropic of Cancer and the Tropic of Capricorn. These two areas are located north and south of the Equator. They are called subtropical zones.

Turkestan

Gobi

Taklimakan

Iranian

Thar

Tropic of Cancer

Sahara

Arabian

e palm tree

Somali-Chalbi

Equator

Namib

Tropic of Capricorn

Great Sandy

frilled dragon

aari

Gibson

kangaroo

Great Victoria

Simpson

meerkat

9

Fab Four

Deserts come in four basic varieties: subtropical, coastal, rain shadow, and interior. Most of the world's deserts are subtropical. Subtropical deserts are caused by the circulation of air in Earth's atmosphere. Hot, wet air rises near the Equator, drops its rain in the tropics, and then flows toward the subtropics. By the time the air reaches the subtropics, it is dried out, so clouds seldom form and rain rarely falls.

Clouds act like a blanket, blocking out heat during the day and keeping in warmth at night. Because deserts have no cloud cover, they bake during the day and cool quickly at night.

LANDLOCKED
Interior deserts, such as the Gobi in Asia, lie in the center of a continent. An interior desert is so far inland that by the time ocean winds reach it, their moisture is long gone.

COASTAL STYLE

[S]outh America's Atacama Desert is one of the world's [t]wo coastal deserts. The other one is the Namib, [i]n Africa. A coastal desert occurs where cold ocean [c]urrents near the shore chill the air, creating fog but [n]ot rain clouds.

CACTUS COUNTRY
North America's Sonoran Desert is a subtropical desert. It stretches from Arizona and California down into Mexico. The Sonoran is the only place where the giant saguaro (seh-WAHR-oh) cactus grows.

rain shadow

rain

rain shadow

[R]AIN ROBBER

[R]ain shadow deserts, such as South America's Patagonian Desert, lie in the [s]hadow of mountains. As wet winds from the ocean rise over a mountain [ra]nge, they cool and drop their moisture on the mountains' sea side. The winds [th]en blow down the other side of the mountain range—the rain shadow— [d]elivering only hot, dry air to the land in their path.

1 Sand and Stuff

Deserts are more than just sand. In fact, sand covers only about one-fourth of the world's arid lands. Most deserts feature a mixture of other surfaces. Wind-scoured, gravel-covered plains pave many dry miles. Salty, sandy, chalky, crumbly, or clay-like soils coat other areas. Dried-up lake beds, called playas (PLIGH-uhz), are also found in deserts the world over.

DUST STORM
Strong winds whip up tiny specks of dust from the desert into swirling storms, then carry the dust thousands of miles.

Barchans (bar-KAHNZ), or crescent-shaped dunes, are created by a constant wind blowing from one direction.

Seif (SEEF) dunes are squiggly shapes made by slight shifts in the direction of the wind.

Star dunes grow where winds constantly shift direction.

Transverse dunes develop at right angles to the direction of the wind.

DUNE DATA
Dunes form when windblown sand meets an obstacle on the desert floor, such as a rock or a plant, and begins to pile up around it. There are four basic types of dunes. The shape of a dune depends on which way the wind is blowing.

ALL CRACKED UP
Playas form when runoff from rare rains settles in low spots, then dries up.

ROWNING IN SAND
...shed by the wind, sand
...nes can travel hundreds
...feet each year. Moving
...nes slowly cover
...ything in their path,
...ch as this farm on the
...ge of the Sahara. This
...adual spread of the
...sert is referred to as
...sertification.

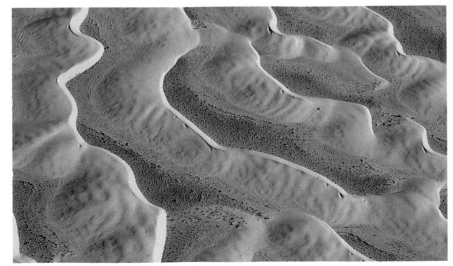

WHITE WONDER
Most desert sand is
made of quartz, but
these sparkling dunes
are made of a lighter,
softer mineral called
gypsum. You can find
them in New Mexico's
White Sands National
Monument in the
Chihuahuan Desert.

13

Fantastic Forms

Talk about out of this world! The bizarre landscapes in some deserts may look like they belong on another planet, but they were formed by nature's tools of wind, sand, and water. Over countless centuries, fierce winds have blasted desert landforms with sand, sculpting them into the spectacular shapes we see today. Rare but powerful rainstorms produce flash floods that also erode, or wear away, desert lands. And deserts have few plants to help anchor the soil.

RED ROCKS
Called Kata Tjuta (KAH-tah TCHEW-tah), these islands of stone stand t: in Australia's desert interior. Scientists believe they were once part of a sandstone plateau, or hig plain. Wind and water wore away the softer sandstone.

SIGHT-SEEING

You can see landforms like these in deserts the world over. Mesas are flat-topped mountains with steep sides. Buttes are smaller versions. Arches are bridge-shaped landforms. Caprock columns are larger on top than at their base. Arroyos, also called wadis (WAH-dez), are deep gullies that were cut into the desert floor by rushing waters from flash floods. They are dry except when it rains.

butte

arch

caprock column

mesa

arroyo

STONE NEEDLES

Rock towers in Utah's Bryce Canyon owe their spiky shapes to wind, water, and ice, which carved away the softer stone and soil that once surrounded them. Their vivid colors come from iron and other metals in the rock. One reason desert landforms look so striking is because their shapes and colors are not hidden under a topcoat of plants. The shapes keep their rugged good looks over time because there is little rain to erode them.

2 Deserts Alive!

Imagine spending day after day under a scorching-hot sun with barely any water to drink for months, or even years, on end. Impossible? Not for desert plants. They have developed special features, called adaptations, that enable them to survive the heat and make the most of whatever moisture there is.

Euphorbias, like cactuses, store water in thick, spongy leaves and stems.

CACTUS COUSIN
Native to African and Asian deserts, the euphorbia plant is similar to the cactuses found in the arid lands of North and South America.

QUICK-CHANGE ARTIST
Most of the time globemallow plants look dead, but they are really just resting until a good rainfall arrives. This inactivity in times of dryness is called estivation (EST-eh-vay-shun).

Within a few days of rainfall, globemallows grow leaves and burst into bloom.

FLOWER POWER
Annual plants, like these wildflowers in the Sonoran Desert, are the most numerous plants in the desert. Annuals spend most of their lives as seeds.

PRETTY PRICKLY
Sharp spines on the prickly pear and other cactuses discourage hungry animals and help protect the plants.

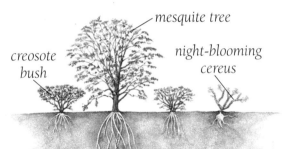

creosote bush

mesquite tree

night-blooming cereus

ANNUAL ANTICS
The seeds of annuals can lie dormant, or inactive, in the soil for decades. When enough rain falls to soak the ground, the seeds sprout. Then the seedlings grow, flower, and produce seeds of their own— all in a few weeks.

This beautiful annual, called Sturt's desert pea, grows in the deserts of Australia.

WATERWORKS
To survive, desert plants need to collect as much water as possible. Mesquites reach as deep as 175 feet to tap into water. Roots of the creosote give off poisons that keep competition away. Cereus (SEAR-ee-us) store moisture in underground bulbs.

Creature Feature

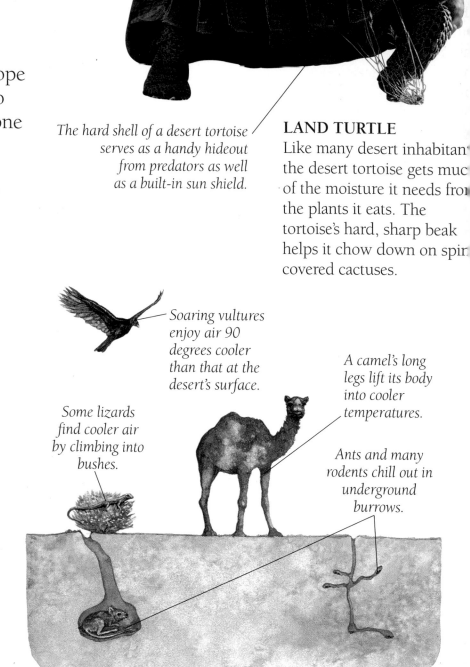

If life is a challenge for plants in the desert, it is no picnic for the animals that live there either. Like plants, desert creatures have to cope with searing heat and lack of water. They also have to find food and avoid becoming someone else's meal. To meet these challenges, desert animals, like desert plants, have adapted in a variety of ways that give them an edge over their harsh habitat.

The hard shell of a desert tortoise serves as a handy hideout from predators as well as a built-in sun shield.

LAND TURTLE
Like many desert inhabitant the desert tortoise gets muc of the moisture it needs fro the plants it eats. The tortoise's hard, sharp beak helps it chow down on spin covered cactuses.

Soaring vultures enjoy air 90 degrees cooler than that at the desert's surface.

A camel's long legs lift its body into cooler temperatures.

Some lizards find cooler air by climbing into bushes.

Ants and many rodents chill out in underground burrows.

OUTFOXING THE HEAT
Desert animals face the problem of overheating. The kit fox of North America solves it by resting in an underground burrow during the hottest part of the day. Its large ears also help it keep cool by letting excess body heat escape through them. The fennec fox of the Sahara relies on the same strategies.

SIZZLING HOT
By midday, the desert's surface temperature can exceed 150°F! Animals find relief from this intense heat both above and below the ground.

18

SHADE SEEKER

During the day a jackrabbit takes it easy in the shade of a plant or rock. In the evening it ranges farther to forage, or search, for food. Like the kit fox, the jackrabbit has huge ears that help it stay cool. It relies on speed to outrun predators.

Long eyelashes and bushy eyebrows help keep sand out of a camel's eyes.

When food and water are scarce, a camel converts the fat in the hump on its back into the nourishment it needs. If a camel goes too long without water, its hump will shrink or sag over.

ONE HUMP OR TWO?

One-humped camels, called dromedaries, are native to Africa and the Middle East. Two-humped camels live in Asia. A camel can go without water for up to ten days. Broad, soft feet help it walk over loose sand. A woolly coat insulates it from the heat of day and the chill of night.

19

Survival Strategies

For some desert animals, the key to surviving dryness is knowing how to wait it out. The eggs of Australia's fairy shrimp, for example, can live in dry lake beds for 50 years. When rain finally refills the lakes, each egg hatches into a tiny larva that quickly grows up, mates, and lays its own eggs before the water dries up again.

Soon after fairy shrimp hatch, birds from all over fly to the lake for a feast.

SAVING FOR A DUSTY DAY
Full of nectar, honey-pot ants called repletes hang from the ceiling of a nest. In wet seasons worker ants gather the sweet liquid from flowers and feed it to the repletes. In dry times, when food is scarce, the repletes nourish the ant colony with their stored nectar.

TWO OF A KIND

The kangaroo rat and the jerboa are not related, but they sure look and act like it. They both hop, eat seeds, and spend the day underground. Each can live its whole life without a drink of water. Over time these two animals have developed similar adaptations to cope with desert extremes.

Kangaroo rats are found in the deserts of North America.

Jerboas make their home in the deserts of Africa and Asia.

ATER BOY

is desert bird, called a sandgrouse, must have fresh ter daily. It flies to water holes to get it. While the le bird drinks, its feathers soak up water like a onge. When it returns to the nest, its chicks sip the ter from its feathers.

SPIKER DUDE

The horned lizard's blotchy colors help it blend in with the desert floor and hide from hungry predators. Camouflage like this is a survival strategy used by many desert creatures. The horned lizard gets more protection from its spiny scales. As a last resort, this ant-eating lizard shoots blood out of its eyes at an attacker.

Day-Trippers

Take a trip to the desert, here the Sonoran Desert of Arizona, and you will see that desert days belong to birds, lizards, and those few mammals that can handle the heat, such as the collared peccary and Harris's antelope squirrel. Even these creatures, however, seek shade or shelter during midday, when the sun glares down and the desert floor sizzles. They hunt or forage for food in the morning or late afternoon. Animals who can't tolerate the heat, such as the kangaroo rat and the tarantula, spend daytime hours in burrows or dens.

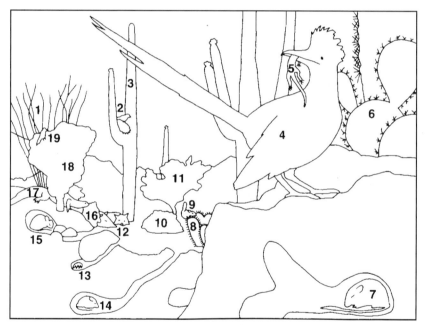

1 Ocotillo
2 Harris's hawk
3 Saguaro cactus
4 Roadrunner
5 Zebra-tailed lizard
6 Prickly pear cactus
7 Desert pocket mouse
8 Hedgehog cactus
9 Harris's antelope squirrel

10 Jimsonweed
11 Foothill paloverde
12 Collared peccary
13 Desert tarantula
14 Kangaroo rat
15 White-throated woodrat
16 Brittlebrush
17 Chuckwalla
18 Teddy bear cholla
19 Cactus wren

Night Club

Nighttime is the right time for many desert creatures. As darkness falls and the temperature drops, animals such as the kangaroo rat, the ringtail, and the tarantula leave the places where they shelter during the day to begin looking for food. Many desert animals are nocturnal (NOK-turn-el), which means they are active at night. Nocturnal animals are more common in the desert than in any other environment.

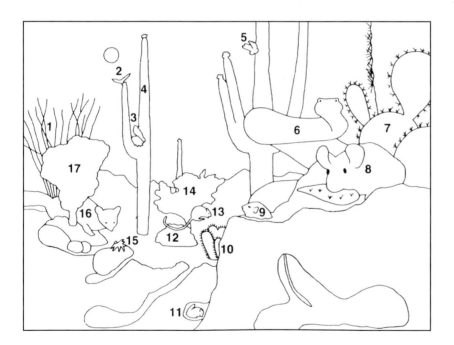

1 Ocotillo
2 Sanborn's long-nosed bat
3 Harris's hawk
4 Saguaro cactus
5 Elf owl
6 Western diamondback rattlesnake
7 Prickly pear cactus
8 White-throated woodrat
9 Desert pocket mouse
10 Hedgehog cactus
11 Harris's antelope squirrel
12 Jimsonweed
13 Kangaroo rat
14 Foothill paloverde
15 Desert tarantula
16 Ringtail
17 Teddy bear cholla

Sahara and Arabian Desert

Stretching across the top third of the African continent, the Sahara is the largest desert in the world. It is so big that all 50 United States could almost squeeze inside it. The Sahara got its name from an Arabic word meaning "desert." A subtropical desert, it contains mountains, dry streambeds called wadis, gravel plains called regs, and vast seas of sand called ergs. Many scientists consider its neighbor, the Arabian Desert, a continuation of the Sahara.

PICTURE PERFECT

Ancient rock paintings show that thousands years ago the Sahara contained enough wate support large game animals, such as buffalo.

Rain falls on one side of a mountain range, trickles down through the soil, and travels underground.

MEGA DUNE

The Arabian Desert contain: largest patch o sand on Earth. Dunes there sc 800 feet high.

GREEN SCENE

Many desert dwellers—including people—depend on oases for drinking water. This Saharan oasis is in the country of Morocco.

MOIST MIRACLE

Islands of green called oases (o-AY-sees) dot the Sahara and other deserts of the world. Palm trees and other plants flourish in oases because water is present year-round. Oases form where water seeps up from underground.

When underground water runs into solid rock, the water flows upward. This creates a pool called an oasis.

Beating the Heat

What a hot spot! Some of the highest air temperatures ever recorded on Earth occurred in the Sahara—more than 130°F! Temperatures on the ground climb even higher. The Sahara is also one of the driest places on the planet. In parts of it the sun can evaporate, or dry up, 200 times more water than falls as rain. What could endure in such a place? A surprising number of things.

Big ears radiate heat away and pick up sounds of prey.

HITCHHIKER

Keeping an eye out for insects to eat, a carmine bee-eater rides on the back of a kori bustard. The bustard's long legs rai it off the hot desert floor, keeping it and its passenger cooler.

COOL CAT

Panting is one way that deser cats, such as this caracal (CARE-ah-call), and other meat-eating mammals get rid of excess body heat. This Saharan cat rests in shade by day and hunts animals its ow size or larger by night.

28

CKING HORNS

o ibex battle it out in the
abian Desert. The winner
ll rule the herd and mate
th the most females. The
ex spends the daytime in
ves or other shady places.
comes out at night to graze
plants. Like humans, ibex
d other antelope-like
atures sweat to cool down.

*To protect its eggs
from desert heat,
the Saharan bird
called the white-
crowned black
wheatear builds a
pyramid of stones
about six inches
tall. Then it makes
its nest on the top.*

29

4 The Foggy Namib

Rainfall in the Namib Desert averages less than one inch a year, but this coastal desert on Africa's southwest shore does get a dose of fog from the Atlantic Ocean almost daily. This fog is the main source of water for many of the plants and animals that live in the Namib, and they know how to take advantage of every tiny drop.

WEBBED WONDER
This spiderweb has snared two treasures: a mot[...] for the spider's supper and precious water droplets.

OLD GLORY
The welwitschia (well-WIT-see-uh) plant absorbs moisture from fog through its strap-like leaves. These plants can live to be 2,000 years old.

Head-stander beetles in the Namib perch upside-down at the top of a dune to gather fog droplets. The drops collect on the insect's body and roll down into its mouth.

BLOOMING ROCKS?
It's easy to see why lithop plants are also called living stones. A pebble-like part of each plant stores water.

Lithops rely on fog's moisture, which rolls off nearby rocks and seeps down to the plant's roots.

ROLLING ON THE RIVER ▶
Swollen by rains in the highland to the east, a river churns throug[...] sand dunes in the Namib Desert [...] Riverbeds in the desert, such as t[...] one made by this river, are usual[...] bone-dry for years on end.

Living Sands

For the beetles and spiders, lizards and snakes that live in the sand dunes of the Namib, life is simply sandtastic! Over the ages, these dune-dwellers have become expert sand-users. Some creatures burrow into sand to escape the scorching sun, for example, and some dive into it to escape enemies. No plants grow on the dunes, but that's no problem for the insects and lizards that live there. They survive by feeding on plant and animal fragments—such as seeds, bits of leaves, or a dead fly's leg—that are blown there by the wind.

WATCH YOUR STEP!
To hide as it waits for prey, a sidewinder viper wriggles down into the sand, leaving only its eyes and nostrils exposed. When a lizard comes near, the snake strikes swiftly.

Strong front claws help the golden mole dig quickly through sand.

DUNE DIGGER
The golden mole follows its nose as it tunnels just below the surface in search of prey, mainly insects. This blind mole can sense vibrations made by nearby creatures. It is one of the few mammals that lives in the dunes of the Namib.

DISAPPEARING ACT
A sand-diving lizard pokes its head out to see if the coast is clear. When alarmed, it plunges snout-first back into the sand.

SAND SKIMMER
Webbed feet help this gecko glide across loose sand and dig into a dune to escape a snake or other predator.

The gecko cleans its eyes with a flick of its tongue.

SLY SPIDER
The white lady spider spins grains of sand into her web, then drapes it over her burrow. When a cricket or other insect walks over the sandy trap, it gets stuck.

To flee an enemy, the white lady spider folds in her legs and cartwheels down a dune.

33

Big Attractions

Elephants in the desert? Sometimes. And they are not the only large animals that occasionally roam the dunes and rocky flatlands of the northern Namib Desert. For moisture, these animals depend on water that remains trapped in sand just below the floor of the region's dry riverbeds.

FATHER KNOWS BEST

An ostrich father guards its chicks and eggs from hungry hyenas and jackals. This big bird releases excess body heat through its extra long legs and neck.

At just two pounds, a meerkat can be easily snatched up by a hawk or an eagle.

GUARD DUTY

Namib suricates (SOOR-uh-kates), also called meerkats, stand watch atop their burrow. If a guard spots a predator, it alerts its den mates. Cooperation such as this helps ensure meerkats' survival.

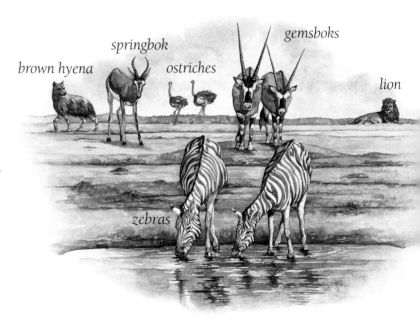

brown hyena   springbok   ostriches   gemsboks   lion

zebras

PIT STOP

Water holes are often dug in dry riverbeds by animals such as gemsboks or elephants, which use their trunks to dig down. In other places, moisture seeps up on its own to create small pools in the riverbeds. Water holes lure a variety of wildlife.

SPIKY SNACK

[A] softball-size
[na]ras fruit
[pr]ovides a
[m]oisture-rich meal
[fo]r a jackal.
[El]ephants, hyenas,
[an]d ostriches in
[th]e northern
[N]amib also feed
[o]n the naras. The
[pl]ant's long roots
[re]ach down deep
[to] find water.

FLOOD FEAST

Plants growing in a flooded riverbed taste great to Namib elephants. These animals can go without water for three or four days. They can travel up to 45 miles a day from one water hole to the next.

5 Asia's Deserts of Extremes

Temperatures in the Gobi and the Taklimakan (tock-luh-muh-KAHN) Desert of Asia are scorching in summer and freezing in winter. Frigid winter weather is why these two arid lands are often called cold deserts. Both the Gobi and the Taklimakan are interior deserts.

GREAT GOBI
Nomads pitch tents and graze animals on dry grasslands called steppes in the Gobi. Most of this desert is covered with pebbl plains. In fact, the word "gobi" means "pebble-strewn plain" in Chinese.

Most pet gerbils in the U.S. today trace their roots back to gerbils brought here from the Gobi in the 1950s.

PEELING PAINT?
Actually, this is a close-up of the Gobi's dry, cracked surface. Parts of the Gobi go years between rainfalls.

LAND OF NO RETURN
That's what the name of the Taklimakan Desert means. Plant and animal life here exist mainly on the fringes of the desert. The heart of it consists of empty sand dunes.

In the winter, the corsac fox migrates south, where prey animals are more plentiful.

The rare Asian wild ass roams the desert in times of rain, when food and water are available.

The hedgehog deals with the cold Taklimakan winter by hibernating through it.

ILD AND
OOLLY
o-humped, or
ctrian, camels
m wild in the
bi. This one has
shaggy winter
t, which it will
d when the
ather warms.
ctrian camels have
gh feet for
ssing rocky land.

37

6 Deserts Down Under

Deserts dominate the land down under, also known as Australia. About two-thirds of the continent is covered with arid lands, which are divided into four main deserts: the Great Sandy, the Gibson, the Great Victoria, and the Simpson. These subtropical deserts consist mainly of vast stretches of sandy soil, stone-covered plains, and low hills and cliffs. Because Australian deserts receive more rain than those of Africa or Asia, more plants flourish there.

IN THE PINK
A pink cockatoo perches in a tree, one of many small species that grow in Australian deserts. These trees provide nesting and feeding places for a variety of different birds.

BLOWING IN THE WIND
Coaxed to life by rain earlier in the season, annual wildflowers called billybuttons sprout from a desert dune. Winds will soon scatter the dried-out flowers' seeds.

Many animals, including, scorpions, spiders, grasshoppers, cockroaches, beetles, and hopping mice, crowd spinifex, a grass unique to Australia.

SEEING RED ▶
Soils formed from red sandstones and granite giv Australian deserts their ric color. Grasses and low shr rooted in the dunes help k them from blowing away.

Leaping Lizards!

When it comes to lizards, Australia wins claws down. Its deserts host some 230 kinds of lizards, more than any other arid land. Lizards down under range in size from inch-long geckos to seven-foot monitor lizards. Most of Australia's lizards are predators. Small ones eat insects. Big ones prey on birds, small mammals, and other lizards.

CHOW TIME
A death adder stretches its jaws around a knob-tailed gecko, which is named for the knob on its tail. Australian deserts are home to a wide variety of snakes, two-thirds of which are poisonous.

SAY AHHH!
The blue-tongued lizard hisses loudly and wags its colorful tongue to scare off enemies. Short legs allow it to slither across sand.

CLIMATE CONTROL
Like other reptiles, the monitor lizard controls its body heat by moving into and out of sunlight. To appear larger and more threatening, it stands upright.

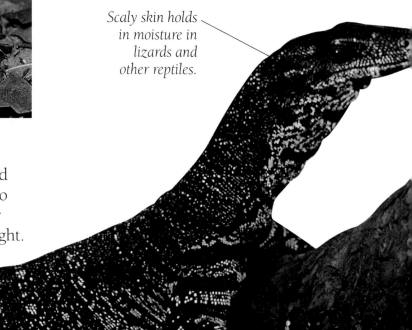

Scaly skin holds in moisture in lizards and other reptiles.

BACK OFF!

To make itself look bigger and more ferocious when a predator threatens, the frilled dragon raises the loose flap of skin around its neck into a stiff collar and opens its mouth wide. Enemies are startled by the display, which allows the lizard to escape by running away on its hind legs.

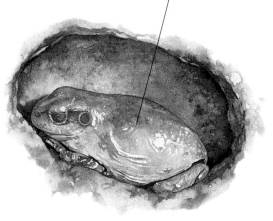

In dry times, the water-holding frog looks as if it is wearing a plastic bag.

SEALED TIGHT

Australia's water-holding frog is one of the few amphibians to adapt to desert life. In between rare rains, the frog buries itself in a burrow and secretes a covering that keeps its body from drying out.

Marvelous Mammals

The deserts of Australia are home to a collection of mammals. Most of them are marsupials. Marsupials give birth to tiny, underdeveloped babies that crawl into a pouch on their mother's chest. The mother carries and nurses her baby in the pouch until it grows big enough to survive outside. Most marsupials need less food than other mammals, which helps suit them to desert life.

The wallaroo inhabits rocky, hilly areas. It can go long periods without water.

The echidna looks like a cross between a porcupine and an anteater. It feeds on ants and termites.

Rabbit-ear bandicoots marsupials live in shall burrows.

POUCH POWER

Australia's deserts are famous for their marsupial inhabitants. But they are also home to the echidna, one of only two egg-laying mammals in the world. Also called the spiny anteater, the echidna lays an egg into a pouch on its body.

The fat-tailed mouse is a marsupial that stores fat in its tail. It eats insects and lizards.

Similar to the golden mole of the Namib Desert, the marsupial mole spends its life underground

The spectacled hare wallaby is a jackrabbit-size marsupial that feeds on plants.

HUNTING DOG
Largest predator in Australia, the wild dog called the dingo sometimes strays into the desert to prey on kangaroos.

The red kangaroo can reach seven feet in height. It is the largest marsupial.

A kangaroo beats the heat by licking its paws. As the moisture evaporates, the animal cools down. It also pants to release heat.

HOP TO IT
Kangaroos, like this big red one, roam Australia's deserts in groups called mobs. They drink water when it is available, but in dry times they get all the moisture they need from the plants they eat.

Deserts American Style

So where's the desert? That's what a visitor from the Sahara might ask on a trip to North America's four deserts: the Great Basin, Mojave, Sonoran, and Chihuahuan. Although these lands do seem green and wet by comparison, they are definitely dry enough to qualify as deserts. The Great Basin is North America's largest desert. It is hot in summer and cold in winter. The Great Basin is a rain shadow desert.

ROOM AND BOARD
Low shrubs, such as sagebrush, grow throughout the Great Basin. Many Great Basin animals rely on sagebrush for food and shelter.

BOSS BADGER
Venturing out for a drink, the badger is normally active at night. That's when this desert predator hunts and patrols its mile-wide territory. Badgers dig through dirt to catch mice and other rodents. To escape from the hot sun, they spend the day in underground dens. Badgers dig a new den almost every day and rarely sleep in the same place twice.

pronghorn

sage grouse

sage thrasher

grasshopper

sagebrush lizard

rattlesnake

SPRING BEAUTY ▶
Fed by melting snow, streams in the Great Basin flow for a short time only in spring. The rest of the year they are dry. Most of the precipitation in the Great Basin is snow.

The mountain lion also stalks South American deserts, where it is called the puma (POO-meh).

TOP CAT
Found in all four North American deserts, the mountain lion is the largest predator in all of them.

Hunting Grounds

The Mojave, Sonoran, and Chihuahuan Deserts are subtropical deserts that are hot year-round. They get more rain than other deserts, so they support a wider range of plant and animal life. And because the majority of animal species in deserts are carnivores, or meat-eaters, there's a whole lot of hunting going on.

BEEP BEEP
The roadrunner prefers running to flying. It races as f[ast] as 20 miles per hour to capture lizards or mice—or t[o] escape from a coyote. Roadrunners are also talented rattlesnake killers.

DEATH VALLEY
Sloping sand dunes and gully-scarred hills dominate the landscape in Death Valley, a region of the Mojave Desert. Death Valley is the lowest, hottest, and driest place in the United States. Ground temperatures there climb above 190°F!

Plants are the bottom link in any food chain. Plants in a given area usually outweigh plant-eating animals ten to one.

TOP BIRD
The golden eagle is a desert bird of prey that is eaten by no other animal. That puts it at the top of its food chain. A diagram helps show what eats what.

LETHAL LIZARD
The gila monster chews venom into its prey, then swallows it whole.

The gila monster's tail stores fat. This lizard lives off that fat when food is scarce.

OTCHA!
scorpion feasts a gecko after ving it a deadly se of poison. The orpion injects nom into victims th a flick of the nger on its tail.

POISON PAL
Nearly as large as a grown-up's hand, the tarantula also has a venomous bite. This spider rests underground by day.

Garden Variety

The desert world's greatest variety of plants can be found in the Sonoran Desert, which generally enjoys some rainfall in both summer and winter. The Sonoran is home to more than 300 kinds of cactus alone, ranging from tiny pincushions to saguaros taller than telephone poles.

Cactus thorns are no problem for a desert squirrel, which uses them as ladder steps.

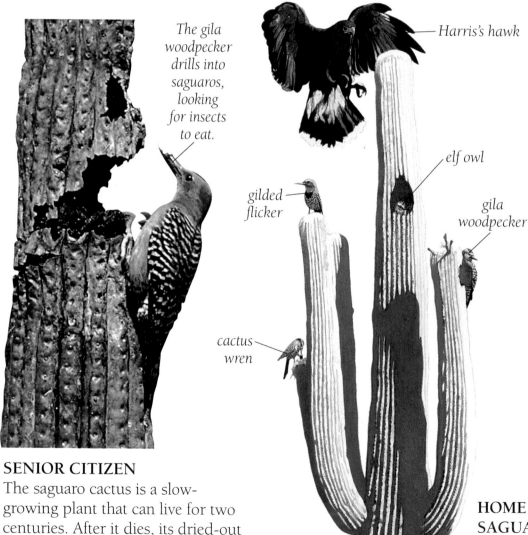

The gila woodpecker drills into saguaros, looking for insects to eat.

Harris's hawk

gilded flicker

elf owl

gila woodpecker

cactus wren

GIANTS AND JUMPERS
Saguaros loom over smaller cactuses called jumping chollas (CHOY-yuhs). At the slightest touch, the cholla's barbed branches break off and stick to passersby.

SENIOR CITIZEN
The saguaro cactus is a slow-growing plant that can live for two centuries. After it dies, its dried-out hulk may stand for years, providing a home for scorpions and termites.

HOME SWEET SAGUARO
Saguaro cactuses provide nesting places for 15 kinds of birds, some of which are featured here.

IT TAKES TWO ▶
Yucca blossoms provide yucca moth with a safe place to lay their eggs. In the process, the moths pollinate the plant.

8 South America's Cool Duo

Pack a parka if you head to South America's Atacama or Patagonian Desert in wintertime. They both get wickedly cold. And don't forget a water bottle. Parts of the Atacama go without rain for decades. The Patagonian Desert gets more moisture, so it has more plant and animal life.

The rhea stands about three feet tall.

CAMEL KIN
Guanacos (gwah-NOCK-ohs) graze on grasses. These members of the camel family can run nearly 35 miles an hour to escape enemies such as pumas.

BIG BIRD
Long, loose feathers protect the rhea (REE-uh), a flightless Patagonian bird, from heat and cold.

Spots and stripes help this wildcat blend into its surroundings.

PRETTY KITTY
Geoffroy's cat may look like a fluffy pet, but it is actually a fierce predator. It hunts birds and rodents in the Patagonian Desert.

ILD AND WINDY
ld winds whip the
eless plains of the
tagonian Desert year-
und. Shrubs, grasses, and
ctuses grow in this rain
adow desert.

When other food is scarce, the Peruvian fox feeds on dead fish, crabs, and seaweed washed ashore by the waves.

THE BAREST OF THEM ALL
Because the Atacama is too dry to have many plants, it supports very limited animal life. The few creatures that do live there, such as the Peruvian fox, tend to eat almost anything.

9 People of the Desert

Desert animals and plants have physical adaptations that help them cope with heat and dryness, but the people who have lived in the world's deserts since prehistoric days do not. Over time, however, desert peoples have developed special clothing, shelters, diets, and ways of life that help them survive.

KEEPING SHEEP
This Navajo woman in Arizona herds sheep, as do many other desert people around the world.

CITY OF STONE
Desert people carved the city of Petra into cliffs in the northern Arabian Desert 2,000 years ago. Inside the cliff dwellings, the temperature is much cooler than outside.

SURVIVAL GEAR

[r]obe and veil protect [thi]s Tuareg man from [dus]t and windblown [san]d in the Sahara. The [loo]se robe allows air to [cir]culate, which helps [his] body stay cool. The [Tua]reg people are [tra]ditionally nomads— [peo]ple who travel from [pla]ce to place. Today, [ma]ny desert nomads [ha]ve moved to [per]manent settlements.

[DI]GGING DOWN

[Pe]ople of the Bushmen tribe live in Africa's Kalahari, a desert south of the [Sa]hara. The Kalahari has almost no surface water for ten months of the [ye]ar. Bushmen get the water they need from juicy fruits such as melons, [an]d by digging up moisture-rich bulbs and roots.

DUSTY DANCING

Dancing in a special ceremony, native inhabitants of Australia, called Aborigines, stir up red desert dust. For at least 30,000 years, Aborigines have relied on their expert hunting skills for desert survival.

10 Dry Ice

No place on Earth is dryer than the continent of Antarctica. The air there is just too cold to hold much moisture. For this reason, Antarctica is sometimes called a polar desert. The Arctic—the region around the North Pole—often gets the same label because it gets so little precipitation. Most of that is in the form of ice or snow.

Antarctica's largest land animal is a wingless fly less than 1/10 of an inch long.

POLAR PALS

Many animals thrive in the Arctic, including polar bears, the largest land animals there. Polar wildlife copes with year-round cold and long, dark periods. Desert creatures face heat and bright light.

DOWN IN THE VALLEY ▶

Although 98 percent of Antarctica is covered with thick ice, winds keep a region known as the Dry Valleys swept to bare rock and sand.